Mango Madness

The Essential Mango Recipe Book

BY

April Blomgren

Copyright 2017 April Blomgren

License Notes

No part of this Book can be reproduced in any form or by any means including print, electronic, scanning or photocopying unless prior permission is granted by the author.

All ideas, suggestions and guidelines mentioned here are written for informative purposes. While the author has taken every possible step to ensure accuracy, all readers are advised to follow information at their own risk. The author cannot be held responsible for personal and/or commercial damages in case of misinterpreting and misunderstanding any part of this Book

Table of Contents

Introduction

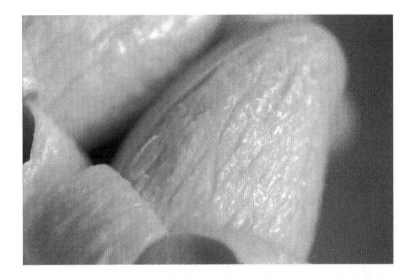

Mango Madness is the taste of Summer and the following recipes will delight you. Packed full of essential vitamins – mangoes are a great source of natural fibre and are a sweet refreshing summer treat. Delight friends and family with the delicious recipes in our mango cookbook.

Mango Pudding

Prep Time 25 minutes

8 Serves

The delicate flavours of mango in this Asian inspired pudding are divine.

Ingredients

- 2 x 15 oz. cans mangoes in syrup
- 5 tsp. gelatine powder
- ½ cup caster sugar
- 2 cups mango nectar
- 1 x 13 oz. can evaporated milk
- double cream to serve
- fresh mango slices to serve

Method

1. In a food processor, blitz the canned mango until it is smooth.
2. Reserve the syrup and place ¾ cup into a heatproof bowl.
3. Scatter the gelatine powder over the syrup.
4. Place the bowl in boiling water and whisk till the gelatine has fully dissolved.
5. In a saucepan, over a low heat, combine sugar and ¾ cup mango nectar until sugar dissolves.
6. Let it cool.
7. Combine the gelatine mix, mango nectar mix and evaporated milk with the mango puree until smooth and creamy.
8. Pour into your serving glasses and cover.
9. Place in the fridge to set for at least 6 hours.
10. Serve with cream and mango slices. Delicious!

Mango Tart

Prep Time 35 minutes

6 Serves

So very easy to make and very delicious – a great inexpensive dessert that is low in calories too.

Ingredients

- 2 mangoes – cubed
- 1 sheet puff pastry
- 4 ½ oz. white marshmallows
- sorbet to serve

Method

1. Preheat oven to 390F.
2. Grease and line a 9 -inch cake pan.
3. Place mango and marshmallows over the base of your pan.
4. Put your pastry over the top and trim off any excess pastry.
5. Into the oven and bake for 25 minutes, until golden.
6. Let is set for 5 minutes and serve it up warm.

Cheeky Mangoes

Prep Time 10 minutes

2 **Serves**

This is like dessert done on the barbecue – also really great with fresh fish!

Ingredients

- 9 oz. mascarpone
- ¼ cup icing sugar
- 1 Tsp. lime juice
- 1 tsp. lime zest – grated
- 2 Tsp. caster sugar
- 2 tsp. basil – chopped finely
- 2 mango cheeks

Method

1. In a bowl, combine the lime zest, lime juice, icing sugar and mascarpone.
2. Place in the fridge, covered.
3. Scatter basil and sugar over your fleshy mango cheeks.
4. Heat up your barbecue over a high flame and chargrill your mango cheeks until they caramelise.
5. Serve up with your mascarpone mix immediately.

Mango Lassi

Prep Time 5 minutes

2 **Serves**

The sweet taste of India – the mango lassi is a taste sensation.

Ingredients

- 1/2 x 15 oz. can mango slices in syrup
- ½ cup Greek-style yogurt
- 1 Tsp. caster sugar
- 1 ¼ cups milk
- Cardamom – ground

Method

1. In a blender, combine mango, yogurt, milk and sugar and blitz till smooth and creamy.
2. Sprinkle cardamom on top.
3. Serve it up fresh.

Mango Chutney

Prep Time 1 hour and 15 minutes

12 **Serves**

The perfect condiment to have on hand – homemade mango chutney is so versatile and delicious.

Ingredients

- 3 mangoes – chopped
- 2 brown onions – chopped
- 1 cup apple cider vinegar
- 2 cups white sugar
- 1 Tsp. fresh ginger – grated finely
- 2 tsp. cumin seeds
- 1 tsp. coriander – ground
- 1 tsp. mixed spice
- A pinch of ground cloves

Method

1. In a heavy based saucepan, over a high heat, bring to boil, mango, onion, sugar, vinegar, coriander, cumin, ginger, mixed spice and cloves.
2. Lower the heat and simmer for 1 hour until the mix thickens.
3. Stir occasionally.
4. Portion chutney into sterilised jars and seal.
5. Let them cool completely and store until ready to eat.

Mango Coconut Cheesecake

Prep Time 6 hours and 40 minutes

10 **Serves**

The three textures of this beautiful cheesecake will leave you wanting more.

Ingredients

- 1 x 8 oz. packet white chocolate and macadamia biscuits
- 1 cup coconut – shredded
- 1 cup butter – melted
- 2 Tsp. boiling water
- 2 tsp. gelatine powder
- 18 oz. cream cheese - softened
- 1/3 cup caster sugar
- 1 tsp. coconut essence
- 3 cups cream

Mango Jelly Ingredients

- 1 ½ cups mango puree
- 1/3 cup caster sugar
- 1 Tsp. lemon juice
- 2 Tsp. boiling water
- 3 tsp. gelatine powder

Method

1. Line the base and sides of a 9 x 2.5 inch round spring form pan with baking paper.
2. In a food processor, blitz biscuits and ½ cup coconut until finely chopped.
3. Pour into a bowl and combine with butter and remaining coconut.
4. Press into the base of your pan to form a biscuit base.
5. Into the fridge to set for 30 minutes.
6. Dissolve your gelatine in the boiling water and set aside to cool.
7. Beat sugar, coconut essence and cream cheese until creamy.
8. Slowly add in cream and gelatine and combine well.
9. Pour the mix over your biscuit base and put into the fridge to set for 4 hours.
10. In a saucepan, over a medium heat, combine mango puree and sugar.
11. Bring to the boil and take off the heat.
12. Pour in juice and stir well.

13. Dissolve gelatine in 2 Tsp. boiling water and add to the mango mix.

14. Let it cool and spoon over the top of your set cream cheese and biscuit base.

15. Into the fridge for 2 hours to set.

16. Serve up fresh and enjoy!

Coconut Prawn and Mango Salad

Prep Time 30 minutes

4 **Serves**

This is such a delicious lunch time meal I love to share with my girlfriends – goes great with bubbly!

Ingredients

- 2 eggs – free range – whisked
- 2 tsp. fresh ginger – grated
- ¼ cup rice flour
- 2 cups coconut – shredded
- 17.5 oz. green prawns – peeled and tails intact
- 1 lime – zest and juice
- 3 tsp. fish sauce
- 2 ½ tsp. brown sugar
- 1 long red chili – sliced
- 1/3 cup coconut oil
- 2 cups bean sprouts
- 1 cup fresh mint leaves
- 1 cup fresh coriander leaves
- 1 mango – sliced
- 1 avocado – sliced

Method

1. In a bowl, mix 1 tsp. ginger and egg.

2. Place the coconut and flour in separate bowls.

3. Dip your prawns into flour, followed by egg and then coconut.

4. Place on a tray while you prepare your dressing.

5. In a bowl, mix lime juice, fish sauce, chili and sugar with remaining ginger.

6. Put to the side.

7. In a frypan, over a medium heat, heat oil and cook prawns until they are golden.

8. Drizzle lime zest over them and season.

9. On a plate, arrange all of your salad ingredients and place prawns on top.

10. Cover with your dressing and serve up fresh!

Mango Chicken Curry

Prep Time 50 minutes

4 **Serves**

There is nothing better than mango in a fresh curry – a delicious meal to share with the family.

Ingredients

- 1 x 15 oz. can mango slices
- 1 Tsp. olive oil
- 35 oz. chicken thigh fillets – halved
- 1 brown onion – sliced
- 1 red capsicum – sliced

- 1 garlic clove – crushed
- 1 tsp. fresh ginger – grated
- 1/3 cup korma curry paste
- 1 x 14 oz. can coconut milk
- ½ cup chicken stock
- steamed rice and green chili to serve

Method

1. Puree your mango slices in a blender till smooth.
2. In a frypan, over a medium heat, heat half of your oil and brown your chicken.
3. Place on a plate.
4. Pour in your remaining oil and cook your onions till tender.
5. Ginger, capsicum and garlic go in next and cook for 2 minutes.
6. Add paste and cook till fragrant.
7. Pour in milk, stock and pureed mango.
8. Place your chicken into the mango mix and bring to the boil.
9. Lower the heat and simmer for 20 minutes.
10. Serve your curry up with rice and chili.

Mango and Pistachio Friands

Prep Time 50 minutes

10 **Serves**

A yummy combination of ingredients in these moist friands
– time for a cup of tea!

Ingredients

- ½ mango – sliced thinly
- 6 egg whites – free range
- ½ cup plain flour
- 1 ½ cups icing sugar
- 5 oz. pistachios
- oz. butter – melted and cooled

Method

1. Preheat oven to 390F.
2. Grease a 10 – hole friand baking tin.
3. In a food processor, blitz pistachios until ground.
4. Pour into a bowl with flour and icing sugar.
5. In a bowl, whisk egg whites until frothy.
6. Fold in your pistachio mix with butter and gently combine.
7. Pour into your prepared pan and place mango slices on top.
8. Into the oven and bake for 30 minutes.
9. They smell so good!

Mango Passion Party Punch

Prep Time 10 minutes

8 Serves

Party time!!! Whip up this tasty punch in no time at all and enjoy the tropical flavours.

Ingredients

- ½ cup mango nectar – chilled
- 3 passionfruit – halved
- ½ cup ginger beer – chilled
- 1 cup pineapple juice – chilled
- 1 bottle of sparkling wine – chilled
- ice cubes and pineapple wedges to serve

Method

1. In a large jug, combine nectar, ginger beer, passionfruit and pineapple juice with the wine and stir well.
2. Serve up in glasses with ice and pineapple wedges. Cheers!

Salmon With Mango And Chili Salsa

Prep Time 25 minutes

4 **Serves**

Protein packed goodness with the good omegas and the fruity flavour of mango.

Ingredients

- 4 skinless salmon fillets
- 1 Tsp. olive oil
- 2 ripe mangoes – chopped
- 1 long red chili – seeded and sliced thinly
- 2 Tsp. fresh coriander – chopped
- 1 Tsp. fresh lime juice
- 1 bunch asparagus
- lime wedges to serve

Method

1. In a frypan, over a medium heat, heat oil and cook salmon to your liking.
2. Combine mango, chili, lime juice and coriander in a bowl and season.
3. Blanche asparagus in boiling water until tender.
4. Place salmon on plates with asparagus.
5. Top with mango salsa and serve with lime wedges.

Mango and Macadamia Nut Turkey

Prep Time 8 hours and 25 minutes

4 **Serves**

So very delicious and so worth the time to create – a special exotic, fruity treat.

Ingredients

- 2 lb. roast turkey breast
- ¾ cup sweet mango conserve
- ½ cup macadamia nuts – toasted and chopped
- 1 lime – zest and juice
- steamed asparagus and roasted potatoes to serve

Method

1. Preheat oven to 370F.
2. Place turkey in a roasting pan and into the oven.
3. Roast for 1 hour.
4. In a bowl, mix conserve, nuts, juice and zest.
5. Take turkey out of the oven.
6. Pour mango mix over your turkey and roast for another 30 minutes.
7. Baste every 10 minutes until the turkey is golden.
8. Remove from the oven and let it stand for 10 minutes.
9. Serve up with vegetables and drizzle with mango sauce form the roasting pan.

Mango and Passionfruit Crunch

Prep Time 15 minutes

4 **Serves**

A beautiful dessert that is so simple to prepare and easy on the wallet.

Ingredients

- 10 Butternut Snap cookies – crumbled
- 1 x 5 oz. can passionfruit pulp in syrup
- 1 x 17 oz. packet frozen mango – diced
- 2 ½ cups thickened cream
- 1 x 5 oz. coconut cream
- ½ cup flaked coconut to serve

Method

1. Take 2 Tsp. of the thick coconut cream from the top of the can and place in a bowl.
2. Pour in the cream and beat until soft peaks form.
3. Portion half of your crumbled biscuit into 4 serving glasses.
4. Place half of your mango on top of the biscuit crumbs.
5. Top with cream mix and passionfruit pulp.
6. Continue to layer until all of your ingredients are gone.
7. Scatter coconut on top and serve up fresh.so yum!

Frozen Mango Margarita

Prep Time 10 minutes

8 Serves

Dreamy frozen margaritas on a hot sunny afternoon – yes please!

Ingredients

- 2 x 11 oz. packets frozen mango cheeks
- 1 cup silver tequila
- 2/3 cup fresh lime juice
- 2/3 cup Cointreau liqueur
- ½ cup caster sugar
- 2 cups ice cubes

Method

1. In a blender, blitz mango, tequila, juice, sugar, Cointreau and ice until creamy smooth.
2. Pour into glasses and serve up fresh.
3. Cheers!

Chicken and Mango Parcels

Prep Time 20 minutes

4 Serves

The kids will love this protein packed meal – tasty and full
of healthy goodness.

Ingredients

- 2 tsp. peanut oil
- ¼ cup soy sauce
- 1 Tsp. lime juice
- 1 lb. chicken mince – free range
- 3 green onions – chopped finely
- 1 mango – diced
- 1 iceberg lettuce – leaves separated
- sweet chili sauce to serve

Method

1. In a non-stick frypan, over a high heat, heat oil and cook your mince until golden, approx. 5 minutes.
2. Pour in lime juice and soy and cook for 2 more minutes.
3. Stir through onions and take the mince mix off the heat.
4. Fold through your mango.
5. Fill lettuce leaves with mince mix and drizzle with sweet chilli sauce.

Oysters with Mango And Basil Salsa

Prep Time 15 minutes

12 **Serves**

A very fancy entrée that tastes exotic and will delight your dinner guests.

Ingredients

- 1 mango cheek – chopped finely
- ½ Lebanese cucumber – chopped finely
- 1 Tsp. red onion – chopped finely
- 5 large fresh basil leaves – torn
- 12 natural fresh shucked oysters

Method

1. Mix together mango, cucumber, onion and basil in a bowl and season.
2. Place your oysters on a serving platter lined with salt.
3. Spoon mango mix onto each oyster and serve immediately.

Mango, Chia and Almond Breakfast Bowl

Prep Time 5 minutes

2 **Serves**

A great start to the day – packed full of energy and the goodness of mangoes vitamin C.

Ingredients

- ¼ cup oats
- 2 Tsp. black chia seeds
- 1 cup almond milk
- ½ tsp. cinnamon – ground
- 1/3 cup natural yogurt
- 1 mango – sliced
- 2 Tsp. almonds – sliced
- cinnamon to serve

Method

1. In a bowl, mix chia and oats.
2. Pour in milk and scatter cinnamon over the top.
3. Place in the fridge, covered overnight.
4. Portion into bowls the next day for breakfast.
5. Place yogurt, mango and almond on top and sprinkle with cinnamon.

Scallops with Fresh Mango And Saffron Sauce

Prep Time 1 hour and 25 minutes

6 Serves

A tasty seafood treat combined with the sweet flavour of fresh mango.

Ingredients

- 2 mangoes
- 2 Lebanese cucumbers
- 1 lime – juiced

- 1 tsp. white wine vinegar
- 2 Tsp. olive oil
- 1 Tsp. fresh coriander – chopped
- 2 ¼ cups white wine
- 2 ¼ cups thickened cream
- 1 tsp. saffron threads
- 36 scallops

Method

1. Slice mangoes into slivers and place to the side.
2. Peel your cucumbers into ribbons and place in a bowl.
3. Pour oil, juice, vinegar and coriander over the top and mix well.
4. In a pan, over a low heat, simmer, wine, cream and saffron until it thickens.
5. Put to the side.
6. Thread scallops onto skewers and oil.
7. Heat a pan, over a high heat and cook scallops to your liking.
8. Serve with mango salad and drizzle with saffron cream – serve up fresh.

Mango Pineapple and Coconut Bread

Prep Time 1 hour and 35 minutes

8 Serves

Morning tea anyone? This bread is moist and full of island flavour.

Ingredients

- 1 ½ cups self-raising flour
- 1 cup brown sugar
- ½ cup desiccated coconut
- 2 cups pineapple – crushed
- ½ cup buttermilk
- ¾ cup butter – melted

- 2 eggs – free range
- 2 bananas – mashed
- 2 frozen mangoes – chopped finely

Passionfruit Glaze Ingredients

- 1 ½ cups icing sugar
- 2 Tsp. passionfruit pulp
- 1 lime – zest

Method

1. Combine coconut, flour and brown sugar in a bowl.
2. In a separate bowl, whisk eggs, milk and banana together.
3. Pour into your flour mix and combine well.
4. Add mango and pineapple, folding gently through.
5. Preheat oven to 370F.
6. Grease and line an 8.5 x 4.5 inch loaf pan.
7. Pour your mix into the pan and into the oven.
8. Bake for approx. 1 hour and turn out onto a wire rack to coll.
9. Make the glaze by combining icing sugar and pulp until smooth.
10. Spread over your cooled loaf and scatter lime zest on top.

Baked Mango and Coconut Rice Pots

Prep Time 1 hour and 20 minutes

4 **Serves**

The kids will love these delicious individual rice puddings with this yummy mango and coconut combination.

Ingredients

- 1 cup milk
- 2 eggs – free range
- 2 tsp. caster sugar
- 1 tsp. vanilla essence
- 2 cups coconut milk

- 1/3 cup white rice
- 1 cup water
- ¾ cup brown sugar
- 1 mango
- 2 Tsp. coconut – shredded

Method

1. Preheat oven to 350F.
2. Grease 4 ovenproof ramekins.
3. In a jug, combine coconut milk, milk, eggs, caster sugar and vanilla.
4. Into each ramekin, place 1 Tsp. rice and pour the milk mix over the top.
5. Place in a roasting dish and fill with boiling water halfway up your ramekins.
6. Place foil over the roasting tray into the oven to bake for 10 minutes.
7. In a saucepan, over a low heat dissolve sugar and water.
8. Simmer into a syrup for about 5 minutes.
9. Place your mango into a blender and blitz till pureed.
10. Pour over your puddings and then drizzle with syrup.
11. Serve up warm.

Mango Melba

Prep Time 15 minutes

4 **Serves**

A summer time treat is mango Melba – served with summer berries and coconut ice cream.

Ingredients

- 4 mangoes
- ¾ cup butter – melted
- ¼ cup brown sugar
- 1 punnet of raspberries
- 1 Tsp. icing sugar
- coconut ice-cream to serve

Method

1. Preheat a chargrill pan over a high heat.
2. Slice the cheeks from your mango and coat with butter.
3. Scatter brown sugar over the flesh and grill till it caramelises.
4. Put to the side.
5. In a blender, combine icing sugar and raspberries and blitz till smooth.
6. Place mango cheeks in serving bowls, scoop ice-cream in and drizzle with raspberry sauce.

Mango Rice Salad

Prep Time 45 minutes

6 **Serves**

A delicious vegetarian rice salad that is perfect for a light lunch.

Ingredients

- 1 ½ cups jasmine rice
- 1 bunch Thai basil
- 1 bunch mint leaves
- 1 bunch coriander leaves
- 1 lemon – juice and zest
- ¼ cup olive oil
- 2/3 cup coconut – shredded
- 6 spring onions – sliced
- 1 long red chili – seeded and sliced
- 2 mangoes – chopped
- ½ cup peanuts – roasted and chopped
- 1 cup shallots – fried
- lemon wedges to serve

Method

1. Cook your rice, drain and rinse.
2. In a jug, whisk oil and juice and season.
3. Chop basil, coriander and mint.
4. In a frypan, roast coconut until lightly toasted.
5. In a large bowl, combine rice, herbs, coconut, zest, chili, mango and peanuts.
6. Scatter with shallots and serve with lemon wedges.

Mango and Macaroon Trifle

Prep Time 1 hour and 15 minutes

6 **Serves**

A delicious, healthy trifle which is not only creamy and flavoursome but also low in fat.

Ingredients

- 1 cup apricot and coconut cookies – crumbled
- 12 sponge finger biscuits – quartered
- 1/3 cup white dessert wine
- 3 cups fat – free custard
- 2 mango cheeks – sliced thinly

Method

1. In an 8-cup capacity serving bowl, place one third of the sponge biscuit.
2. Pour one third of wine over the top and then top with one third custard.
3. Your mango goes on next.
4. Repeat the process until all ingredients are used up.
5. Into the fridge, covered for an hour and then spoon into bowls.

Mango Lychee and Coconut Terrine

Prep Time 4 hours

8 Serves

A tropical summer time sweet treat – delight your dinner guests with this refreshing terrine.

Ingredients

- 24 lychees – seeded
- 7 cups mango sorbet – softened
- 3 cups coconut cream
- ½ cup coconut chips – roasted
- lime zest to serve

Method

1. Line an 8 x 4-inch loaf pan.
2. Slice your lychees in half and mix with sorbet and coconut cream in a bowl.
3. Pour into your prepared pan and cover and freeze.
4. Serve up with coconut chips and zest.

Sweet Sticky Mango Rice

Prep Time 25 minutes

6 **Serves**

A delicious rice dish you can even dish for breakfast.

Ingredients

- 1 cup short grain rice
- 3 cups water
- ½ cup white sugar
- 1 ½ cups coconut cream
- 3 mangoes – sliced

Method

1. In a saucepan, combine rice and water and bring to the boil.
2. Lower the heat and cook for 10 mins.
3. Pour in coconut cream and simmer for another 5 minutes.
4. Serve in bowls with fresh mango and the remaining coconut cream. Yum!

Author's Afterthoughts

Thanks ever so much to each of my cherished readers for investing the time to read this book!

I know you could have picked from many other books but you chose this one. So a big thanks for buying this book and reading all the way to the end.

If you enjoyed this book or received value from it, I'd like to ask you for a favor. Please take a few minutes to post an honest and heartfelt review on Amazon.com. Your support does make a difference and helps to benefit other people.

Thanks!

April Blomgren

About the Author

April Blomgren

Hello everyone! Are you ready to grill tonight? My name is April and I love to cook and entertain friends and family almost every weekend. If you share my passion for great food, easy preparation time but mouthwatering results, you and I are going to get along just fine!

I think a successful meal among loved ones is based on a few key factors: fresh ingredients and appropriate cooking method. Some meats for example, can truly benefit from being marinated overnight, and will be at their best prepared on the grill. Another aspect of cooking I must insist on, no matter what your cooking style is: rely on the use of herbs and spices. Please favor fresh herbs each time you can. However, I understand that it may be difficult during certain periods of the year, so simply keep a well-stocked pantry of dried basic herbs and spices such as cinnamon, nutmeg, basil, oregano, thyme or any other favorites.

Finally, once you embark that exciting culinary journey with me, you will realize that simplicity is also one of my allied. Don't overthink when cooking. Inspire yourself of recipes, have fun doing it and taste as you go. Sure, you might once in a while burn a few pork chops or use too much salt in your sauce, you are just human. Cooking is not about succeeding every time, it is about the opportunity to learn and get better. Don't be afraid to taste your dishes along the way, adjust the seasonings and serve accordingly.

REYN

REYN
+507 6979 -0906

Made in the USA
San Bernardino, CA
15 September 2019